DINOSAURS!

CETIOSAURUS
AND OTHER DINOSAURS AND REPTILES FROM
THE MIDDLE JURASSIC

by
David West

Gareth Stevens
Publishing

Please visit our website, www.garethstevens.com.
For a free color catalog of all our high-quality books,
call toll free 1-800-542-2595 or fax 1-877-542-2596.

Library of Congress Cataloging-in-Publication Data

West, David, 1956-
Cetiosaurus and other dinosaurs and reptiles from the middle Jurassic / David West.
p. cm. — (Dinosaurs!)
Includes index.
ISBN 978-1-4339-6709-2 (pbk.)
ISBN 978-1-4339-6710-8 (6-pack)
ISBN 978-1-4339-6707-8 (lib. bdg.)
1. Cetiosauridae—Juvenile literature. 2. Paleontology—Jurassic—Juvenile literature. I. Title.
QE862.S3W4655 2012
567.9—dc23
2011031676

First Edition

Published in 2012 by
Gareth Stevens Publishing
111 East 14th Street, Suite 349
New York, NY 10003

Copyright © 2012 David West Books

Designed by David West Books

Special thanks to Dr. Ron Blakey for the map on page 4

Printed in China

CPSIA compliance information: Batch #DW12GS: For further information contact Gareth Stevens, New York, New York at 1-800-542-2595.

Contents

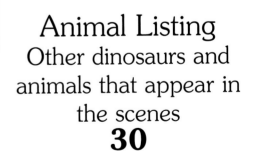

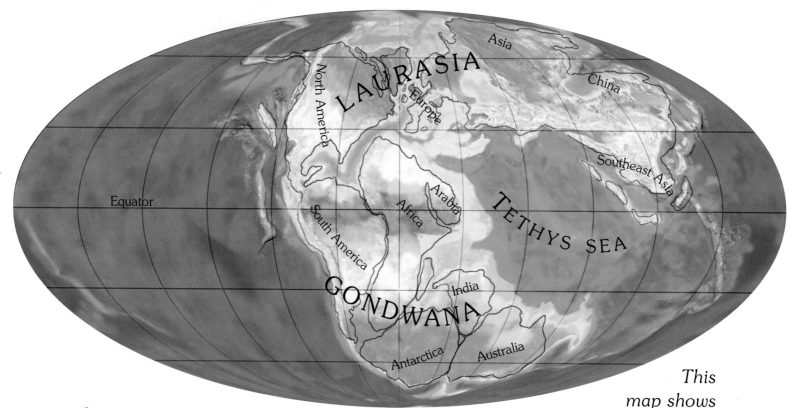

This map shows what the world looked like around 170 million years ago.

The Middle Jurassic Period

As the Earth's plates continued to shift apart, shallow seas close to land became more widespread. The **monsoon** weather pattern of the Lower Jurassic broke down and some areas became drier, especially in Laurasia. Conifers were dominant, and other plants, such as **ginkgoes**, **cycads**, and ferns, became more numerous. As the climate improved, new species of dinosaurs and other reptiles evolved.

*Dinosaurs lived throughout the Mesozoic Era, which is divided into three periods, shown here. It is sometimes called the Age of Reptiles. Dinosaurs first appeared in the Upper Triassic period and died out during a **mass extinction event** 65 million years ago.*

Some new dinosaurs took to the air.

Giant reptiles and fish lived in the oceans.

LIFE DURING THE MIDDLE JURASSIC

In the air, this period saw the last of the long-tailed **pterosaurs**. New forms of dinosaurs appeared, including very small feathered dinosaurs that could glide from tree to tree. The long-necked dinosaurs started to increase in diversity and numbers as the **prosauropods** died out. Some of the **sauropods** grew extremely long necks. Many dinosaurs and reptiles lived on the coasts, especially in what is today Europe, where the water had swamped the land, creating a shallow sea dotted with islands. The oceans became home to some of the largest reptiles yet seen as well as the biggest fish ever!

227	200	180	159	144		98		65 Millions of years ago (mya)
Upper	Lower	Middle	Upper		Lower		Upper	
TRIASSIC		JURASSIC			CRETACEOUS			

Giants and Hunters

The **fossils** of a large sauropod were found in the Atlas mountains of North Africa. Named after its place of discovery, *Atlasaurus* is one of a few sauropods to have roamed Middle Jurassic Africa.

This giant dinosaur had the longest legs of any recorded sauropod. Its front legs were much longer than its back legs, giving it an unusual profile. It is considered to be closely related to *Brachiosaurus*, a North American sauropod from the Upper Jurassic period. Living at the

6

A pair of Afrovenators (1) *have caught a young* Chebsaurus (2) *on the plains of what is today Africa. A family of* Atlasauruses (3) *gather around their young to form a protective screen against the* Afrovenators.

same time in North Africa was another sauropod called *Chebsaurus*. The fossils of this dinosaur are believed to be from a **juvenile** measuring 30 feet (9.1 m) long. **Preying** on sick and young sauropods was a large **megalosaurid** called *Afrovenator* that grew to be 30 feet (9.1 m) long. This **predatory** meat eater had a mouthful of sharp teeth and three claws on each hand.

Atlasaurus grew up to 50 feet (15.2 m) long and weighed around 16.5 tons (15 metric tons).

7

1

More African Giants

Roaming the continent of Gondwana in what is today Africa were some of the largest animals of the Middle Jurassic. These were sauropods, and the fossils of the biggest yet found were of *Jobaria,* which stood 15 feet (4.6 m) high at the hip.

A range of fossils from adults to juveniles were found, suggesting *Jobaria* may have lived in large herds. Tooth marks on the ribs of a juvenile show that these giants were preyed upon by the top **predator**

A herd of Jobarias (1) *bellow in fear as a pair of* Afrovenators (2) *race in front of them. They are desperate to join their pack member who has just been delivered a powerful blow by the spiked tail of a* Spinophorosaurus (3).

of the time, *Afrovenator* (see pages 6–7). This **theropod** would also have preyed upon other sauropods such as *Spinophorosaurus*. However, it may have found this sauropod a little less easy to bring down. *Spinophorosaurus* had an unusual defense against predators. It had four large spikes on the end of its tail called thagomizers, which it used like a war club.

Jobaria grew up to 59 feet (18 m) long and weighed around 20 tons (18 metric tons).

The Land of Oz

Rhoetosaurus is one of the best known sauropods from Australia. As sauropods go, *Rhoetosaurus* was medium sized, only around 50 feet (15.2 m) long and around 22 tons (20 metric tons) in weight.

Rhoetosaurus might have looked like the late Jurassic *Camarasaurus*, with a fairly long neck but comparatively short tail. Some **paleontologists** believe that *Rhoetosaurus* had a spiked club-like tail similar to the Chinese sauropod *Shunosaurus*, but there is no fossil

On a river in what is now Australia, a small herd of Rhoetosauruses (1) *panic as a group of* Ozraptors (2) *ambush a young member of the herd.*

evidence to prove this. *Rhoetosaurus*, like all sauropods, was a browsing plant eater living in herds of adults and juveniles. It may have eaten the leaves of conifers, seed ferns, and ferns, which are all known from the Jurassic of Australia. Only known from one partial leg bone, *Ozraptor* is difficult to classify. Paleontologists think it may have been an **abelisauroid** theropod dinosaur.

Ozraptor grew to 7 feet (2.1 m) long and weighed, at a guess, up to 1,000 pounds (454 kg).

11

1

2

Gondwanan Hunters

Below a smoking volcano in what is today South
America, a small **heterodontosaurid** called *Manidens*
chases after a group of plant-eating **cynodonts**.
Manidens was probably a **herbivore** but may have
supplemented its diet with meat.

Manidens is the only heterodontosaurid discovered in South America.
Its name means "Hand Tooth," after its hand-shaped teeth. Hunting
bigger game in the forests and plains of Gondwana was a large 23-foot

12

In the foreground, a Manidens (1) *sprints after a group of* Massetognathuses (2) *who run for their lives. Behind them, two* Condorraptors (3) *stalk a* Volkheimeria (4) *feeding on the edge of a forest.*

(7 m) predator called *Condorraptor*. It was a genus of megalosaurid theropod dinosaur, not, as its name suggests, a member of the **raptor** family. Walking on two legs, this meat eater was probably an efficient hunter, preying on young and weak sauropods such as *Volkheimeria*. At 30 feet (9.1 m) long, *Volkheimeria* was fairly small for a sauropod.

Manidens grew to 30 inches (76 cm) long and weighed 10 pounds (22 kg).

Forest Giants

Patagosaurus was one of South America's largest sauropods from the Middle Jurassic. It resembled the English sauropod *Cetiosaurus* (see pages 16–17). It ate plants and was able to stand on its back legs to reach the top branches of tall trees.

Amygdalodon was another South American sauropod of similar size. Its name means "Almond Tooth" because of its almond-shaped teeth. Sauropods spent most of their time feeding on the tough needle-

14

A Patagosaurus (1) *feeds on the upper branches of a forest tree accompanied by an* Amygdalodon (2). *In the foreground, a* Piatnitzkysaurus (3) *disturbs a pair of pterosaurs and a* Massetognathus (4) *as it stalks the sauropods.*

shaped leaves of conifers. Their giant size would have been a good defense against **carnivorous** predators. However, there is evidence of one meat-eating theropod that may well have preyed on these mighty dinosaurs. Its name was *Piatnitzkysaurus*, and it was about 14 feet (4.3 m) long. It had strong jaws filled with sharp teeth and powerful arms with which to grasp its prey.

Patagosaurus grew up to 50 feet (15.2 m) long and weighed 15 tons (13.6 metric tons).

A European View

Europe during the Middle Jurassic was a group of islands in the shallow part of the Tethys Sea. Some animals would have been able to **migrate** across the seas to different islands as they searched for fresh feeding grounds.

Large sauropods such as *Cetiosaurus* and *Cetiosauriscus* would have had no difficulty in crossing the shallow seas between islands. These giant dinosaurs browsed on the lush vegetation using their long necks

A small flock of Rhamphorhynchuses (1) *fly back to their roosts in the evening as a pair of* Proceratosauruses (2) *look down on a coastal plain. A herd of* Cetiosauruses (3) *become agitated as three* Poekilopleurons (4) *run after a sickly* Cetiosauriscus (5).

to reach the upper branches of tall trees. Following the herds were packs of carnivorous dinosaurs such as *Poekilopleuron* and *Proceratosaurus*. These fast-moving predators would have hunted the sick and the young of the sauropod herds. Feeding on fish and amphibians, *Rhamphorhynchus* flew far and wide across the European islands.

Rhamphorhynchus was about 1 foot (30 cm) long and weighed around 5 pounds (2.3 kg).

17

European Coast

The carnivorous dinosaur *Eustreptospondylus* wandered the islands of Middle Jurassic Europe. It preyed on plant-eating dinosaurs and picked up **carrion** like the dead **carcasses** of marine reptiles such as **plesiosaurs**.

Eustreptospondylus might have encountered marine **crocodyliforms** such as *Teleosaurus*. It was approximately 10 feet (3 m) long and used its long, thin snout filled with sharp teeth to catch fish and squid. It would occasionally come onto land to scavenge off carrion and to lay

On an island coast, a Eustreptospondylus (1) *drags a dead* **ichthyosaur** (2) *from the water. Drawn by the scent of blood, a* Teleosaurus (3) *approaches while two* Sarcolestes (4) *lick salt from rocks. In the background, a lost* Lexovisaurus (5) *wanders the shore.*

eggs. Making rare visits to the beach, *Sarcolestes* was one of the earliest armored dinosaurs. Paleontologists believe it may have been an early type of **ankylosaur**. *Lexovisaurus* was one of the earliest European **stegosaurs**. It had plates as well as spikes protruding from its tail and shoulders. These may have been used to regulate its temperature as well as to defend against predators.

Lexovisaurus was about 20 feet (6 m) long and would have weighed around 0.5 ton (0.45 metric ton).

19

Little and Large

One of the most well-known dinosaurs from the Middle Jurassic was a large carnivore called *Megalosaurus*. Fossil remains of this "Great Reptile" were discovered in the 17th century in England, but it wasn't until the 20th century that paleontologists could accurately portray what it looked like.

Hunting along the shores and forests of the islands of Jurassic Europe, this fearsome predator would have hunted sauropods such as

A pack of Iliosuchuses (1) *bother a* Megalosaurus (2) *in a concerted attempt to snatch pickings from its meal. The dead dinosaur it is feasting on is a* Callovosaurus. *The members of the* Callovosaurus *herd (3) are running for their lives.*

Cetiosaurus (see pages 16–17) and primitive **iguanodonts** such as Callovosaurus. Growing to a modest 11.5 feet (3.5 m) in length, these plant eaters were easy prey to such a large and aggressive dinosaur as Megalosaurus. Competing for meat at a smaller scale were packs of Iliosuchuses. Paleontologists think that they were an early **tyrannosaurid**.

Megalosaurus was about 39 feet (12 m) long and weighed around 1 ton (0.9 metric ton).

21

3

Asian Forest

Amongst the pine forests of Middle Jurassic China lived some of the strangest sauropods. They had extremely long necks to enable them to feed on the highest branches of the tall pine trees. These sauropods, such as *Omeisaurus*, had an amazing 17 neck bones.

Numerous fossils have been found of these giants, which could grow to a whopping 50 feet (15.2 m) in length and weigh up to a massive 10 tons (9 metric tons). Living around the same time was

A tree splinters and falls as an Omeisaurus (1) *crashes to the ground during a territorial contest with another long-necked dinosaur called* Eomamenchisaurus (2). *A* Monolophosaurus (3) *will kill the injured dinosaur when the rest of the herd leaves.*

Eomamenchisaurus. This long-necked sauropod may have competed with *Omeisaurus* for the same food. Skirting the edges of the herds of these giant dinosaurs were large predators such as *Monolophosaurus.* This **allosaur** was bigger than *Dilophosaurus* and had a single crest along its nose that was probably used for display during mating rituals.

Monolophosaurus grew up to 18 feet (5.5 m) long and weighed around 1,500 pounds (680 kg).

23

Clubs and Spikes

Wandering the plains and forests of Middle Jurassic China were herds of an unusual long-necked dinosaur. *Shunosaurus* was small compared with other sauropods, but it had an excellent form of defense—a club on the end of its tail.

The only other sauropod to have a similar defense was *Spinophorosaurus* (see pages 8–9), although it had a set of spikes at the end of its tail. Predators such as *Gasosaurus* could be seriously

A Gasosaurus (1) *looks on as its mate gets thwacked by the tail club of a* Shunosaurus (2) *protecting a juvenile. Two* Huayangosauruses (3) *feed on ferns as a pair of* Angustinaripteruses (4) *fly overhead.*

injured if they were caught by the tail-lashing club of a *Shunosaurus*. Smaller plant eaters such as *Huayangosaurus* developed a similar defensive approach with large spikes growing from the end of their tail. *Huayangosaurus* was a stegosaurid with plates growing out of its back. Scientists think they may have been used to regulate its temperature as well as to frighten off predators.

Shunosaurus was around 33 feet (10 m) in length and weighed about 10 tons (9 metric tons).

Flyers and Gliders

Some of the most unusual dinosaurs started to appear during the Middle Jurassic. Tiny dinosaurs with feathers, such as *Anchiornis* glided between trees using their arm and leg feathers like wings.

Anchiornis was not a bird, although its name means "Near Bird." It represents a link between dinosaurs and the first birds. It had long flight feathers on its arms, hands, and legs. Its long tail was also covered with long feathers. Paleontologists think the feathers on its

26

A *speedy* Darwinopterus (1) *launches an attack on a screeching* Anchiornis (2), *which is gliding between trees of an Asian forest during the Middle Jurassic. An* Abrosaurus (3) *turns to watch the midair action.*

legs would have made it difficult for it to walk easily and suggest that it would have spent most of its time living high up in the trees. This would have afforded it protection from predators, but it may well have been prey to the 2-foot (60 cm) *Darwinopterus*. This flying reptile had a long beak filled with sharp teeth and would have taken prey on the wing.

Anchiornis was only 1 foot (30 cm) long and weighed around 2.2 pounds (1 kg).

27

Ocean Giants

Prowling the seas of the Middle Jurassic was the giant plesiosaur, *Liopleurodon*. Most plesiosaurs had long necks and small heads like *Cryptoclidus*. *Liopleurodon* was a member of the pliosaurids, a suborder of predatory plesiosaurs with large heads and short necks.

Like all sea reptiles, *Liopleurodon* had to surface to breathe air much like modern killer whales. It would have preyed on large fish and other plesiosaurs. One fish it might have avoided was *Leedsichthys*. This giant

A Liopleurodon (1) *attacks a* Cryptoclidus (2) *that has been feeding on* **ammonites** (3). *In the background, a* Leedsichthys (4) *dwarfs a* Metriorhynchus (5) *diving for squid. Deep-diving* Ophthalmosauruses (6) *swim after fish between the coral reefs of this shallow sea.*

was possibly the largest fish ever, reaching a length of 72 feet (22 m). Despite its size, *Leedsichthys* was not dangerous. It was a filter feeder like modern basking and whale sharks. Marine crocodyliforms such as *Metriorhynchus* spent most, if not all, their lives out at sea. They would have lived and hunted alongside the fast-swimming ichthyosaurs such as *Ophthalmosaurus*, whose large eyes were well adapted to the dim light of the oceans depths.

Liopleurodon grew up to 33 feet (10 m) long and weighed around 2.5 tons (2.3 metric tons).

Animal Listing

Other dinosaurs and animals that appear in the scenes.

Abrosaurus
(pp. 26–27)
Sauropod dinosaur
30 feet (9.1 m) long
Asia

Afrovenator
(pp. 6–9)
Theropod dinosaur
30 feet (9.1 m) long
Africa

Amygdalodon
(pp. 14–15)
Sauropod dinosaur
50 feet (15.2 m) long
South America

Angustinaripterus
(pp. 24–25)
Pterosaur
5.2-foot (1.6 m)
wingspan
Asia

Callovosaurus
(pp. 20–21)
Iguanodontian dinosaur
11.5 feet (3.5 m) long
Europe

Cetiosaurus
(pp. 16–17)
Sauropod dinosaur
59 feet (18 m) long
Europe

Chebsaurus
(pp. 6–7)
Sauropod dinosaur
30 feet (9.1 m) long
Africa

Condorraptor
(pp. 12–13)
Theropod dinosaur
23 feet (7 m) long
South America

Cryptoclidus
(pp. 28–29)
Plesiosaur
13.1 feet (4 m) long
Ocean

Darwinopterus
(pp. 26–27)
Pterosaur
2 feet (60 cm) long
Asia

Eomamenchisaurus
(pp. 22–23)
Sauropod dinosaur
72 feet (22 m) long
Asia

Eustreptospondylus
(pp. 18–19)
Theropod dinosaur
9.8 feet (3 m) long
Europe

Gasosaurus
(pp. 24–25)
Theropod dinosaur
13 feet (4 m) long
Asia

Huayangosaurus
(pp. 24–25)
Stegosaurian dinosaur
15 feet (4.6 m) long
Asia

Iliosuchus
(pp. 20–21)
Theropod dinosaur
5 feet (1.5 m) long
Europe

Leedsichthys
(pp. 28–29)
Fish
72 feet (22 m) long
Ocean

Massetognathus
(pp. 12–15)
Cynodont
1.6 feet (50 cm) long
South America

Metriorhynchus
(pp. 28–29)
Crocodyliform
9.8 feet (3 m) long
Ocean

Omeisaurus
(pp. 22–23)
Sauropod dinosaur
50 feet (15.2 m) long
Asia

Ophthalmosaurus
(pp. 28–29)
Ichthyosaur dinosaur
13.1 feet (4 m) long
Ocean

Piatnitzkysaurus
(pp. 14–15)
Theropod dinosaur
14 feet (4.3 m) long
South America

Poekilopleuron
(pp. 16–17)
Theropod dinosaur
30 feet (9.1 m) long
Europe

Proceratosaurus
(pp. 16–17)
Theropod dinosaur
14 feet (4.3 m) long
Europe

Rhoetosaurus
(pp. 10–11)
Sauropod dinosaur
50 feet (15.2 m) long
Australia

Sarcolestes
(pp. 18–19)
Ankylosaurian dinosaur
10 feet (3 m) long
Europe

Spinophorosaurus
(pp. 8–9)
Sauropod dinosaur
42.6 feet (13 m) long
Africa

Teleosaurus
(pp. 18–19)
Crocodyliform
10 feet (3 m) long
Ocean

Volkheimeria
(pp. 12–13)
Sauropod dinosaur
30 feet (9.1 m) long
South America

Glossary

abelisauroid Member of the *Abelisaurus* family of carnivorous theropod dinosaurs.

allosaur Member of the *Allosaurus* family of carnivorous theropod dinosaurs.

ammonite An extinct marine animal with a shell that looks similar to today's nautilus.

ankylosaurs Members of the *Ankylosaurus* family of armored, plant-eating dinosaurs.

carcasses The bodies of dead animals.

carnivorous Meat eating.

carrion The remains of dead animals.

crocodyliforms Group including crocodilians and their extinct relatives.

cycad A kind of palm.

cynodonts A group of therapsids with mammal-like features that laid eggs.

fossils The remains of living things that have turned to rock.

ginkgo An unusual nonflowering plant that is regarded as a living fossil that first appeared in the Lower Jurassic.

herbivore Plant eater.

heterodontosaurid A member of the *heterodontosaurus* family of small dinosaurs known for their canine-like tusks.

ichthyosaur Sea reptile resembling a dolphin.

iguanodonts Members of the *Iguanodon* family of plant-eating dinosaurs.

juvenile An individual that has not yet reached its adult form.

mass extinction event A large-scale disappearance of species of animals and plants in a relatively short period of time.

megalosaurid Member of the *Megalosaurus* family of carnivorous theropod dinosaurs.

migrate To journey from one place to another, either for a short seasonal period or forever.

monsoon The rainy phase of a seasonally changing weather pattern.

paleontologist A scientist who studies the forms of life that existed in earlier geologic periods by looking at fossils.

plesiosaur Marine reptiles with long necks and flippers.

predatory The behavior of a **predator**, an animal that hunts and kills animals for food.

preying Hunting.

prosauropod A member of a group of long-necked, herbivorous dinosaurs that eventually dropped down on all fours and became sauropods.

pterosaur A flying reptile.

raptor Bird-like, carnivorous dinosaurs with large scythe-like claws on their feet.

sauropod A member of a group of large plant-eating dinosaurs that had very long necks.

stegosaurs A group of herbivorous dinosaurs with plates and spikes along their back and tail.

theropod A member of a two-legged dinosaur family that included most of the giant carnivorous dinosaurs.

tyrannosaurid Member of the *Tyrannosaurus* family of carnivorous theropod dinosaurs.

Index

4618